Enjoy!

Chanan Getraide

I'll Take You There

I'll Take You There

Landscapes and Love Verses

Photographs by *Chanan Getraide*

Poems by *Yoram Taharlev*

Cordinata Publishing House

Translated from the Hebrew by *Isadora Cohen*

First published in Hebrew by MOD Publishing House, Israel

Printed in Israel

An Invitation to Love

This is a book for lovers.

There was a time when love was somehow linked to the landscapes that nurtured it, a time when much of romantic poetry described how love bloomed in the bosom of nature. Reading love verses written long ago, one could think that all the beautiful landscapes of my country were created for the sole purpose of providing the perfect setting for love to flower.

This book is an invitation for today's lovers to return to the wondrous landscapes where love once blossomed — the love of generations past, the love of the Biblical heroes.

Come, my beloved, let us go forth into the field
Let us lodge in the villages...
There I will give thee my loves.

Song of Solomon

Looking at these landscapes today, we find them still fresh and alluring, untouched by time.

Every landscape and its magic.
Every tree and its fragrance.
Every blade of grass and its melody.
Every hour of the day and its blaze of colors.
Every season and its charms.

For those lovers who wish to visit these magnificent places from afar, I have written the beginning of a new romantic poem for every one. It will be up to each of you to complete the poems and thus create your own landscapes of love.

Yoram Taharlev

SPRING

Almond trees flowering near Jerusalem

The almond blossom
Comes before the leaves
Beauty before fruit.

The Forest of Angels, northern Negev

Childhood meeting youth
Like wisdom on young branches
In life's passages.

The Jordan river flowing into the Sea of Galilee

All the rivers run into the sea;
yet the sea is not full;
unto the place from whence the rivers come thither they return again.   *Ecclesiastes 1:7*

Motorboats on the Sea of Galilee

If we meet again
I hope we leave behind
Two fading trails of light.

Spring on the Golan Heights

Will the dark shadow
Lurking in the heart of the forest
Veil Spring's innocence?

The Forest of the Holy, near Jerusalem

The almond tree is waiting
For a sudden burst of light
To reveal its natural beauty.
Will love shed its light on me
When the time is right?

In the desert near Mitzpe Ramon

Bloom under old trees
Brings back ancient, haunting ghosts
Of their Cheerfulness

Flowers cover the ancient catacombs of Beit Govrin

Yellow blooms with red.
Can we learn to separate
Jealousy from love?

The mountains of the Judean Desert, north of Massada

I, like the desert,
Under this pale winter sky
Bloom only for you.

Along the coast of the Dead Sea

Water, smooth pebbles,
Wild flowers, peaceful surface
Remind me of you.

The Dead Sea region

Is the greater gift
Mountains' ancient glory or
Magnificent spring?

Spring comes suddenly to the Negev highlands

What lies past that hill?
Follow the desert's arrow there
While your heart's in bloom.

Beauty does not fade
Not if you can see your dream
In the rainbow's wake.

Agricultural lands in the Hula Valley

Sunlight on the field
Spreads the petals wide, but you
Open up at night.

The Negev highlands

Not on tall mountains.
Seek love in ancient canyons
Where streams once ran wild.

SUMMER

The Forest of Angels, northern Negev

At dusk
The timeless blends with the ephemeral
And we take the beaten path.

A shepherd and his herd in the northern Negev

With the herd in tow
Let the shepherd rest
Then walk a mile in his shoes.

The Galilee highlands near Safed

Pine trees and old bench
Know that we shall meet today
Under deep blue skies.

On the way to Eilat

Our roots interlaced
Clouds of love over your head
And I, at your feet.

The agricultural fields of Kibbutz Mishmar David

The field, bare and free,
Now reveals the high tension
Between you and me.

The Judean Desert and the Dead Sea

Sprawling by the water
Under summer's hazy skies
Hills bake in the sun.

The Dead Sea

With days of glory gone
See how lonely and forlorn
The salt of the earth.

Agricultural fields overlooking the Sea of Galilee

Storms and winds will blow
But not harm the crops which grow
Near the precipice.

Sunrise over the Hula Valley

There is no new thing
under the sun.

Ecclesiastes 1:9

Sun rises on hills
And sets in the sea
You see our world's
    age-old ways.

A foggy morning in the Northern Galilee

Whether dusk or dawn
Rising dust or setting sun
Love always shines through.

The Dead Sea Canal

Quench your thirst for love
But have strength to suffer through
Barren aftermaths.

In the Negev highlands near Mitzpe Ramon

See them light and pale
White clouds, white hills, ever white
Wings of my desire.

Wheat fields in the Northern Negev

The Lord is my shepherd I shall not want.   *Psalms 23:1*

Fields of sunflowers in the Lahish region

In this man-made world
Be yourself! Don't ever lose
The wild streak of the weeds.

The Northern Negev

Will this be my life?
Manicured and orderly
Without Love's soft touch?

The Jerusalem-Jericho road

AUTUMN

On the way to Eilat

For the tree of the field is man's life.   *Deuteronomy 20:19*

An orange grove on Kibbutz Shiller

Rays between dark clouds
Know that I shall fear no harm
While I am near you.

A foggy morning in the Galilee

In the sea of love,
Storms, like foam on coffee,
Hide sweetness underneath.

The Dead Sea region

Thou, which hast shewed me great and sore troubles,
shalt quicken me again,
and shalt bring me up again
from the depths of the earth.   *Psalms 71:20*

Along the coast of the Mediterranean

White sands, once pristine,
Still feel night's bold wheels,
                    which marred
Its virginity.

The Judean Desert

These pure, pale blue hills
And my impure, sinful thoughts
Stretch out at your feet.

The Dead Sea

Spare your rueful smile.
For self-love and loneliness
Oft go hand in hand.

On the Egyptian-Israeli border

Make your own bold way.
Dare! For one must never let
Sleeping passions lie.

The Potash Conveyor near the Dead Sea

I remember thee, the kindness of thy youth, the love of thine espousals,
when thou wentest after me in the wilderness, in a land that was not sown.   *Jeremiah 2:2*

Timna Nature Reserve Park

Near the Mediterranean coast

Reality lies.
Even mirrors are islands
Of uncertainty.

The Judean Desert

Turn not left nor right.
But the heart, rebellious, cries:
I shall find my way!

On the way to Eilat

The Mediterranean Sea

High water, wind and foam,
Shadows of a brewing storm,
Can't wash love away.

The Hula Valley

In the glistening rain
Only true lovers can see
Cupid's gaudy bow.

The Golan Heights

The heavens declare the glory of God and the firmament
showeth His handiwork. *Psalms 19:1*

Bental Lake on the Golan Heights

Mountain in the lake.
Reflecting in your tear
                    drops
I see my heartache.

A forest in the Carmel Mountain Range

A time to plant and a time to uproot.   *Ecclesiastes 3:2*

Wonders never cease.
Tiny green leaves are alive
And tough logs are dead.

An almond orchard in the Jezreel Valley

Come, my beloved, let us go forth into the field; let us lodge in the villages.
Let us get up early to the vineyards; let us see if the vine flourish,
whether the tender grape appear,
and the pomegranates bud forth; there will I give thee my loves.

Song of Solomon 7:11

A nature reserve in central Israel

Flowers behind thorns.
Like our parents' tenderness,
Blooming through their years.

An apple orchard in the northern Galilee

Who conceals your thoughts
But your blushing cheek, which tells
What you do not know.

Water flowing into the Jordan River

Many waters cannot quench love, neither can the floods drown it;
if a man would give all the substance of his house for love,
it would utterly be contemned.   *Song of Solomon 8:7*

Wheat fields on the slopes of Mt. Gilboa in the Jezreel Valley

In farming — or in love -
Trust providence, yet know that
Irrigation helps.

Flowers blooming in the northern Negev

He maketh me lie down in green pastures.
He leadeth me beside the still waters.
He restoreth my soul. *Psalms 23:2*

The cyclamen bloom in the Carmel Forest

Like the upright trees,
Can love stand tall on the slope
Beautiful and strong?

An apple orchard on the Golan Heights

Shadows masquerade
While the roots
wait patiently
Hiding in the snow.

Snow in the Galilee

or with every passing day, but also from hour to hour, as if illuminated by a light, which varies from second to second. Nevertheless, the pursuit is an integral part of the game, attempting to catch it in at the precise moment, at which time it is caught totally unaware.

The truth is that a lot of time is spent devising ways how to become a part of this on-going game between light and landscape. The rules of the game are clear-cut and familiar to both players; light fully aware of the absolute control it exert on space, teasingly plays with landscape at whim, as its changes its angels of illumination from morning to evening, until the landscape is totally concealed from sight. The landscape, recognizes the light's control over it, and plays its role on the logical assumption, that if you are illuminated, you do not exist. The landscape begs for attention by changing its colours from tranquility, subdued at times, to turbulence and aggression.

In trying to evaluate nature's phenomena through the eye of camera, it seems that it appreciates man's intervention in the landscape, relishing the modifications introduced by him. As a result of man's intervention new elements are added to the environment, such an electricity poles, roads and abandoned quarries — all of which if seen through the lens of a camera, may be most exhilarating. The camera takes for granted the fact that the finished product will be viewed as would a photograph and not as you might view landscape in nature. I tend to agree with this philosophy as we scan a photograph with a different set of codes than we would a landscape in nature.

Standing before creation, the last rays of daylight lingering, I focus the camera's lens on a strip of landscape with a purpose of capturing it on film at the right moment, snatching it from its natural environment and take it home. Knowing I am allowed to do so — as I have the essential permission. I review the picture one last time, eliminating what seems unnecessary in the frame. I can move that tree over to the left, wait for that dense cloud to enter and let several rays of sunshine filter through to reach the effect and then finally I press the camera's release before it's to late.

With self-satisfaction, I collect my equipment, put it into my bag, fold the tripod, get into my car and drive off. In the rear view mirror, I suddenly catch a glimpse of the sky for which I should have waited a few more minutes... Once again, I am outwitted by the landscape's elusive nature.

A Matter of Landscape   Chanan Getraide

This book is dedicated to my parents, Isha and Adi
To Zofia
To Karny, Maayan, Galit and Hagar

Chanan

Here I stand, facing the landscape set so generously before me and I find myself contemplating whether and to what extent I am free to frame a segment of what I see. In doing this, I have caused a separation between what I have chosen to frame and its natural environment. Does such an act violate Nature's creative rights? Who can one ask? Who is representing Nature itself? As yet, I have not even begun to physically cut and remove the desired piece of landscape from its natural place; I have just captured its image and copied it on film. Meanwhile, world over man is busy physically destroying segments of Nature's creation; whole nations and people are daily obliterating large areas of landscape as they see fit, leveling the folds of the earth, felling its forests, diverting the courses of rivers, rending the skies with huge building and smoke stacks, and totally changing the original landscapes beyond recognition.

As for myself, I feel quite comfortable, in the midst of such reality. I embark on a rendezvous with nature, at which time indulging in preliminary discourse, thus preparing me for what I have set out to do. Only now I am ready to make the first incision. With Nature's guidance, I establish the layout, from which I will hopefully achieve the wholeness of the landscape I am seeking. I watch the shades of colour, the cloud position above and the infiltration of light. And if in times my visit is in vain, I bid farewell, returning at a later date, or perhaps in different season. The landscape is accustomed to this, as it know me well. No less familiar am I with the landscape, and find it not quite as disciplined as I was led to believe. We tend to see the landscape as "still life", an inert object incapable of eluding the watchful eye of the camera. In reality this is not so. Its colours change, inseparably, not only with the changing seasons